Love. Life. And the Pursuit of Acceptance

A Book of Poems

Edward Raniola

authorHOUSE®

AuthorHouse™
1663 Liberty Drive
Bloomington, IN 47403
www.authorhouse.com
Phone: 1-800-839-8640

First published by AuthorHouse 12/16/2010

ISBN: 978-1-4567-1051-4 (sc)

Printed in the United States of America

Any people depicted in stock imagery provided by Thinkstock are models,
and such images are being used for illustrative purposes only.
Certain stock imagery © Thinkstock.

This book is printed on acid-free paper.

March of the Glass Statues

Walking east on a one-way west
Being shoved by all the rest
Living statues made of glass
See through their dirty looks as they pass
Can't blame them though for their manners
For they are going toward a world of hammers

It's not easy to turn against the crowd
Hold your head high and stand proud
Their envy isn't easy to hide
A thick film on their faces resides

They'll try to turn you around
Some with smiles, some with frowns
They make sure to hurt your pride
With each attempt to turn your stride

You'll have to break some to stay on your course
You don't wish to, but to turn would be worse
You won't try to defend your choice
Hoping they'll hear your silent voice

The ability to turn is in their hearts
That's the key to exit their fatal march

Doubt

So you
find
yourself
fallen.
At the bottom
of a well.
Consumed
by darkness.
Just a whisper
of hope
hovers overhead.
A star
from the depth.
An exit
at the surface.
A mirror in your heart.
Mangled in the
cold,
wet dirt.
Internals
mud.
Flashes,
slideshows,
fragments.
A speck.
The star.
Are
your eyes
opened?
Are

you looking
up?
Are
you standing?
Mud pillow.
Fear blanket.
Did you sleep?
Were you here for
long?

Performer

I have to fall out of sight now.
Shall I continue to live this way,
as I die, I'll have to take a bow.

Fear

Our dark partner is cast alongside us.
Our shared limitation
assured. Indiscriminately
placed among us all.

Hopeless Chant

Acid melting away
the sanity. For just a moment
comfort set in.
Bubbles and juices
of which was once
skin. Fumes rise
suffocating me with myself.
Harder to see
with these bloodshot
swollen eyes.
That lost child
found, by way of tears that flow inside.
Boiling into steam
that will surely spew.
Attempt to conceal this furious expulsion.
Gone is the man
the lost child became.

Traveler

I have travelled as a boy in a world of men
As a man in a world of boys
As an observer in a world of people
As a lover in a world of hate
As a sinner in a world of faith
I have broken my word
I have cursed the Gods
Lost my honor and swallowed my pride
I have given up though only inches behind
I have failed to believe
I have much more to see

Just Another Tragedy

Imprisoned in this social play.
Surrounded by actors.
Searching for some new way.
Narrow minds, the horror.
No matter where I look, I see bars
keeping me locked in.
How can anyone reach the stars,
individuality forbidden?
Spike your hair up straight,
fix your face.
Don't be late.
Contain your fear.
Choose a career.
The curtain closes,
the day has ended.
Dream impossibilities
because tomorrow you'll awaken.
Prepare yourself for what the director will be
taking.

A Night Out Amongst Friends

Smiling through these
feelings so incomplete.
Laughter so horrifying
it leaves you sore.

Tear a hole into this skull
and deep within you will find
the source. Crying, screaming rage
blankets empty hopes.
Crisscrossed, tangled decisions intertwined.
Knotted hearts of loss,
and fear to believe
or achieve.
Balanced on a beam, between
two false hopes, and
the glass is half empty.
Fall to an uncertain end.
Smiling and laughing
without ever baring.
Dreaming of sleeping and
awaking, after-life.

And the conversation goes on
without a trace.
In terror from laughing,
never removing the smile from the face.

Paint Each Day

A blank stare reaches
into the depth of
a white canvass.
Black paint begins
across the length
to brighten the surface.
Lines form to
new attitudes.
Connecting blackness through
white hope.
A hint of soothing
creates some green.
Blue smears light to
find the top.
The day forms
early with orange
rise.
Colors next are
known only by one
and for
others,
surprise.

Small Intentions

Sometimes
I feel like breaking down walls.
Sometimes
I feel like talking to pretty girls.
Sometimes
I feel like singing in public.
Sometimes
I feel like taking life for granted.

Surrender

We have to look deep inside.
Find who it is we are trying to hide.
We have to nurture those desires
in order to free the marionette from the wires.
We have to fear nothing within us,
however unique, with or without acceptance.
There will be those that ridicule.
The weak frightened minds that envy you.
It's the majority from which we'll part.
Us being the ones that surrender our minds
to follow our heart.

The Way Things Are

Endings are sad.
People get mad.
Endings can be great,
or not.
Letting go of something familiar,
finding something else to fill you.
Why do things happen this way?
It's the same as a boat rocks in the bay.
Nature has such a funny way
of letting you know just what to say.
Goodbye, hello
my love, just go.
Ups and downs all the time
and you wonder why people turn to a dime-
Bag all the things that will hurt you the most.
Don't let yourself become a ghost.
When you find yourself down and out
don't go through life with a pout.
Smile
and hold your head up high.
Soon love's wings will enable you to fly.
Endings are sad.
People get mad.
Endings can be great,
or not.

Trickery Device

I hate the simplicity in failure.
How easy it is to give up.
Take something for granted.
Quit.
Why can't we
embrace beauty
instead of exploit it?
Why can't we
look into eyes
instead of through them?
Why cant we
accept imperfections
instead of despise them?
Are we incapable of love?
Is love just another religion?
An invention
to assist in control.
A trickery device?

Who Was I

I'm lost in this garden!
Misguided by poisonous flowers.
Infected by ignorance that will never fade.
Encompassed by elder giants
sustaining my miserable existence,
blocking out shining hope.

Smells remind me of who I was.
Colors of who I was.
Sounds. Who I was.
Soft poisonous petals.
Who was I?

A Pull

And now there's this emptiness
residing in my soul.
It needs to be nourished,
it's taking control.
My potential is threatened.
Emptiness filling my mind.
Obsessed with thinking.
My emotions unwind.

Son

hue of our rising giant
do not cast your power
to disturb my blissful moment
in darkness
success lingers in shadows
drawn shades
out of reach of your massive strength
brightening my pseudo world
exposing my despair

Edge

if we forget who we are
can we find us?
if we lose our principles
are we worse off?
can the evil that lives within all
of us surface, take control
and ruin us? all of the good
we once shared lost forever because
we're scared.
a rock's fingerprints are it's edges,
smoothed by the ocean's constant
presence. can we be molded
out of our beliefs, and become what we
despised?
or were we always that, and tried
to hide. the choices we make
determine our pride. we all, to ourselves,
lied. there's just one thing to hope:
in the end,
we're left with some edges.

Flickering

Locked in a cage
Page after page
No way out
No way to win
Afraid it's going to amount to nothing
We are all wicks
Some longer than others
We're all prime for the pick
All sisters and brothers
For some the wind is strong
Puts out the flame fast
Others flicker on

Taking forever to pass

How the Path Split

They're telling us lies!
They say what to do.
They say stay in school.
They say don't try to fight.
They say it wouldn't be right.

What do they know?
In what time did they grow?

They say follow the majority,
those that are secure.
They say forget about spontaneity,
but what if we're unsure?

How can you think you know what we feel?
Tell us the dreams we have can't be real.
What if we don't choose your way?
Does that make us failures?
Such disappointment in your face,
don't you see that scares us?

They say we'll get used to it.
Why should we have to!
We're not you!

They say they just want the best for us.
Do they really think we don't want success?
They say what about him, or her.
They say look, they achieved.

Well I say he or she is not me!
If I do it your way, it's only myself i'll deceive.

They won't understand,
just like we won't give in.

Lone Sensations

As the day turns
to night,
I sit alone
and dream.
Desolate
dreams haunt my night time
peace. Not alone
but so full of living.
Torn
at the seam.
Blue skies wake me to the sound of the alarm.
The trees have changed colors
yet again. The wind brings me
some comfort,
sharing my time throughout the day.
Work,
then to work,
only to work
at something
unknown.
Smiles for the undeserving.
Laughs through the bars
of my cell. Mindless aspirations
shouted courageously.
Night time leaves,
again
a new color.
There is a pattern
to this season
of the day.

Number 6

LOVE
what is it?
LOVE
consuming
LOVE
ruining
LOVE
when do we lose it?
LOVE
sadness
LOVE
forgiveness

Pathetic Irony

You'll look around and forget
your problems.
Realize what more
is in this day.

Understand,
enjoy,
smile.

The sun's up.
A mother giggles with her
child.

You breath in.
You're walking.
Writing.
Reading.
Thinking.

And you couldn't be more depressed.

Baby

Bright light welcome me to Life
Warmth and comfort are my past
My tiny shadow cast
Over disinfected floors
Entering the arms of my first stranger
Passed along and poked and wiped
Awkward faces greet my fear
Smiles and laughs follow my cries

Little miracle created

Quiet tenderness of these familiar arms
Wrapped tight against her chest
Her beating heart beats now for me
My first comfort and first sleep
I know you but how
Blurry woman caring so delicately
A voice that sang me to dreams

Smile of an Uncertain Hope

My awkward smile acknowledged
a meeting of eyes.
Brief.
As was our time.
Tripping over these intentions,
I fall forward to past memories.
Longing for our eyes to meet
again for the first time.

Excited with uncertainty,
we smiled.
Unaware of the moments
we would share.

There was no cold night
lying next to you.
No hope unrealistic.
No dream impossible.

My hand was never empty.
My heart not clenched.
Sweet perfume of your presence
made me want to savor
every breath.

Yet now,
I smile the broken smile
of one lost
in the memories,
of hope and dreams.

The Longest Nights

Before she and I:
My world was fueled by dreams.
Aspirations always failing, every night
ended in a cry.
Imagination wild, I would smile
to myself.
Myself. Myself.
No hand to grasp
or body to hold.
No warm emotion to keep me
from the typical cold.
So long, so longing. I
so full of fear. Asking the sky
to reach down. Asking for
some cure for my frown.
The longest nights are those
alone. Unbearable thoughts
of those around you with love.

Then:
The sky was blue.
We met. Our eyes at first,
then social meeting. Stumbling
over words. Love's hurdles.
All these thoughts, all these lonesome thoughts
gone.
She was my air;
every breath, oh so fresh.
She was my sky;
even when gray the blue would stay.

She was my rain;
bringing life to me as if a lilac or lilly.
She was my soul,
she kept me whole.
She was my smile,
she made me wild.
She was my life,
I wanted her to be my wife.

...

She was my pain.
Eternal, that moment in the rain.
She was gone.

Smothered by every fragrance, every...
breath. What kind of sadist could
bring about her death.
Black skies consumed my world.
Sleepless nights.
Locked away days...every picture...
I wanted to hurl. I wilted
as a flower would in the cold,
without the sun or warm body to hold.
Broken within. Jagged, shattered pieces
tearing at my soul. Sharp as the diamond
over the empty hole. Unbearable
thoughts, of all around you with love.
The longest nights are those alone.

The World Stops

My soul
My beauty
My only salvation
My entrance to life

Reality blurs, fades into fantasy
Your hands smooth and warm
Your lips inviting me
Your eyes sunrise

The stars are replaced
You shine for them all
Rotation has been seized
And gravity falls

Love is defined
A great wind

My entrance to life

Troubled

i want to listen to the voices in my head. Ghosts
haunting my brain. i want to let go of the things
that are dead. Move on to a new terrain.
Darkness stained my mind. As my evil was
framed.
i'll look in the mirror again, what will it reflect? my
self-afflicted neglect. Not hearing, not seeing,
not understanding the world; is not wanting to
realize, not caring, not seeing the dirt on this
pearl.
Zombies with cellphones plugged in our ass.
Non-fat-grande-mocha-latte always within grasp.
The fuel for surviving this social disease. Or you
cry alone on your hands and knees. Numb,
scared, scarred, forgetting. Selling yourself.
Those without a price are placed on a shelf.

Nothing worse than being pitied by those that are
pitiful. Those eyes.

The feeling's mutual.

Aging

fallen angels tarnished and broken
nothing left but an expired token
an expired body
an expired mind
an expired soul
destined to wrong themselves
amongst the bottom of this hole
searching for possibility
discovering reality
immortal guilt in a mortal body

Horror Show

i wake up everyday
in horror
this life is...

i've lost this war
i want to conform
i hate being different
such heartache
i guess we all learn
to go with the pack
i'm a hyena
howling like a wolf
i have to conform
its all thats left
tight shirts, muscles, fast cars
cell phones, career
i pray for a quick death
now
stab me shoot me even
strangle
just do it before i give up my struggle

Exit Ordinary

blue HAIR
PINK nails
moHAWK
TATtoos
does it make you strange?
spike COLLAR
RIPPED jeans
combat BOOTS
CHAins
are you in need of a change?
khaKIS
SWEATers
nah, exit ordinary

Blurry Vision

When all is lost let yourself fly.
Let yourself be.
Don't you see it was never me.
I can't hold on. I'm losing grip.
The iceberg was hit,
and it's sinking the ship.
I want to forget,
I really do.
I want to love life,
but my vision is skewed.

Humanity Come Clean

We're all forms of artificial intelligence.
Designed and running on programed responses.
A laugh, a cry. A smile, or tears.
Can't understand why we have certain fears.
Humanity is only an idea.
What exists now is unclear.

We hate, we hurt, we kill each other.
Wrecking balls swinging through life hitting one another.

We will create humanity,
only it will shine through from machinery.
A robot programmed to love true.
A loyalty that can not be construed.
Friendships that through the years will last,
never looking down on one another
because of color or class.
Competition will no longer run through minds.
Greed and selfishness will be left behind.

It won't be long however, until humans realize
that this manufactured loyalty can be used to take lives.
For if we can create a robot to love true,
we can surely create one to hate too.

So in the end it will be understood:
Human nature chooses power over good.
We're simply a disease
expanding and destroying what we please.
There's no cure at all.
This disease is terminal.

The Ocean of Love

She pulls you into her vast unknown.
She wants you there with her.
You float in to her with ease.
She and you are alone.

Then she crashes down on you.
Pushing and shoving you away,
but you thought she wanted you to stay.
The force of her push knocks you down.
Tumbling, lost. She's nowhere to be found.
You stand up again and search around.
Why has she done this?
You're upset and scared.
You won't leave,
you'll just stand there,
wait for her and plead,

Come back again!
Let me feel you pull me in.

If only you knew,
would you have come here
for her to push and pull?
Does she care she left your heart not full?

I'll leave, just give me one more try.
I'll die here
lost in your ride.

Then it starts,
here comes the swell.

Pull me in,
all is well.
I want to go to your unknown.

In she pulls again,
comfort within your heart.

Wait my friend!

Tumbling, lost,
tired, sore,
You'll pay the cost
to feel her pull you some more.

Is it worth the torment?
Mental and physical anguish.
Maybe you'll leave her and her game.
You'll walk away, towards the insane.
Towards the world where
too many people are fake.
Too many people want more and more to take.
At least she pushes you away
before your soul and love
completely fade.

Plot

i want this ticking to stop
red river flow no more
sadistic night life gleefully trapped in darkness
sun breaks realization with an alarming ring
currents carry listless parts to life
long to have the earth fed
me
plant seeds at my rock
life grows on

So that this Love was There

So that this love was there
And never to be remembered
With how she couldn't care
Led death in November

So that the cold was common
Pain and hurt to be
Souls of those forgotten
Lost without she

The four will pass though
Fade how she never should
Leaves and grass again grow
As new memories could

The Longest Poem

shattered lives blend
giving birth
broken hearts
mend false connections
lost pieces empty spaces
repeat

Thoughts

What did I do? SAVE YOU
for what, for who.
GIVEN ALL
for what, for who.
Confusion
is what
I didn't
know
of
it. I did
though, still hold on
to the feeling. The beginning.
STRANGE
how the beginning was the end.
IRREVERSIBLE

under the SHELL

eVENTUALLY
yOU'LL HAVE TO CONFORM
uNLESS YOU'RE ABLE TO LET GO OF
the norm
pACK INTO THE GYM
yOU'LL HAVE TO BUFF UP
lOSE THE INDIVIDUAL WITHIN
eND UP A HALF EMPTY CUP

yOU THINK YOU'RE BETTER
tHEN THE OTHERS
tHOSE THAT SHINE UNIQUE COLORS
sO SAD YOU CAN BE THIS OBTUSE
wITH AGE YOU'LL REALIZE
oBJECTS RUN OUT OF USE
i KNOW INSIDE THERE'S AN INDIVIDUAL
tHAT WANTS TO EXPRESS
tHEMSELVES FOR REAL
aND WHEN YOU FINALLY COME OUT OF
YOUR SHELL
You'll realize the UNIQUE are pretty swell.

Another Waste

these observations of myself
through strangers in the outside world
a curious child's fascination with ordinary
mundane objects reflects my curiosity
in the parallels of human emotions

Crying Realization

So what! We shared a couple of years
So what! We learned each others fears
Who cares how intimate we were
Who cares if all else was a blur
Forget about those nights together
Forget about returning my old sweater
It won't keep the cold from me
Consider it a lover's fee

So

What happened to your embracing eyes
What happened to our long goodbyes
Why did we drift apart
Why is there an ache, still, in my heart
How can it be this end rearranged us
How can it be we've become strangers
Was it wrong to have loved so much
Was it wrong to have longed for your touch

Good luck I guess, in your search for someone
new
I hope whoever it is will love you

Eyes of the Storm

The light tapping rhythm
against the window soothes
the restlessness of he
as the storm takes him to dreams.

Deep growl of a beast unknown
rattles through his small bones,
too young to understand the storm.

Overjoyed crowds dancing ritualistically
as the soaked sky storms down on them
after a long drought.

Devastation engulfs hearts
of those widowed by the storm.

Ruined time falls, crashes, and lights up
her families vacation in the form of a
thunderstorm.

With options gone from their winter
night, as snow piles their roads, they ignite
a fire and cuddle the storm away.

Generation Next

In order to be accepted we need to change.
We can't be different, only the same.
Don't judge a book by it's cover someone once said.
Well that and the golden rule are as good as dead.

Broken homes, broken hearts,
and children witness it from the start.
Off to Dad's for a few days,
then back to Mom's. How strange.

Father's busy working hard
and Mother's now search for a job.
The child in between it all,
how can we expect he or she to be an individual?

Searching for acceptance. (Where ever it may be.)
It's in the group of drug abusers unfortunately.
Fear
to drugs
to hate
to ruin
disables the children from choosing.

Hypocrite

When are we going to stop this?
Or am I just a hypocrite?
I hate these damn trends!
But I know I'm full of...

Kids are walking around
all drugged up,
blaming society for their troubles.
They don't realize that THEY are society,
and they are the trouble.

And when I'm victim to the trends,
or sometimes an accomplice,
I try to justify my actions
and camouflage my ignorance.

We all have our reasons,
and we all have our vices.
I just wish I could control
life's devices.

Lost Treasure

My heart quivers as I lie next to you,
your eyes infinite,
pulling me in.
You might as well program me.
Although you already have.
I'm yours for this, whatever you want.
I'm your slave. Just
promise me
we can lie together, as we are now,
all nights.
Till our skin turns
gray and wilts, our bones brittle,
our muscles weak.
Till the quivering of our heart stops,
and our souls lift off.

One in All

silence the beast within
to be saved.

one among all.
examine the world with the same eyes.
reach out your hand,
caress the world with the same fingers.
survive with one heart.
inhale
and taste the world with the same tongue.
our tears.
our fears.
our losses.
our gains.
our love.
our peace.
our world.

awaken the hope within.
to save.
to be.

Ponder

question life question rules question society
question limits question reality
question dreams question questions
question answers question potential

question what you don't understand
question what you do understand
question all those around you
strangers family teachers friends
question who you are
question why you are
question that which drives you
question your invisible scars
question that which you love
question that which you hate
question the reasons

question your fate

Social Decay

Pseudo watch, pseudo car.
Let's go to a club,
let's go to a bar.
Plastic body, altered face.
Not an ounce of originality in this place.
Everyone's tough,
acting rough.
Why do we settle for this?
Why do we let it control us?
Dress codes,
endless roads.
Does it really matter
whether my shirt has a collar?
What are we creating,
clones incapable of imagination.
Mirror images.
How sad our society is.
A bird with no wings,
a marionette with no strings.
No longer precious
that first kiss.
What went wrong,
what did we miss?
No one has a care,
drop some E,
drink some GHB,
and no one will be aware.
Social decay.
No one will be spared.

The Miner

Mining for gold
Deep
In darkness
All I see is what's in front of me
The blackest coal
Every attempt
Suffocates my lungs

Is this gold worth it?

The longer I dig
The less familiar I become
Hands darkened, unrecognizable
Face invisible, blending with the blackness
Transforming

Are my eyes even open?
What's in front of me?
Will I even be able to recognize gold?

In this place gold can't exist
My doubt is blackness all around
Engulfed with dark realization

Digging, changing, losing time
Losing myself, losing hope
All effort wasted

I turn from the wall
The dim light
My dying battery reveals

Is it gold?

Lean in close
Behind the bars
Slumped in peace
The yellow canary lies
Color still vibrant

Through Destruction

Her eyes fire.
Engulfing my mind,
heating my soul,
burning through to my heart,
destroying my structure.

Her lips smoke.
Taking my breath,
altering my perception,
adding flavor to my mouth,
intoxicating my emotions.

Her heart savior.
Taking me away from destruction,
cleansing my body,
rebuilding my heart,
healing my wounds.

View from a Box

Wasting, rotting,
decomposing.
Black shirt, black tie.
Black slacks, all dressed.
All black for the event.
The event of a life.
Smiling up at the sobbing.
Just as fake,
(as fake as it was
when they smiled back.)
Can't move in this box.
I never wear a suit.
Empty, hollow,
gutted. Even my heart.
More sobbing.
All these flowers.
My allergies aren't affected.
What a waste. So quick to wilt.
All that color and beauty.

Clarify

You know how you get lost in the stars
of the night sky?
Well that's how I feel
when I look into your eyes.
Are you sure we didn't once meet?
Perhaps another world,
or in a dream?
On impulse I grabbed your hand,
without a thought or worry.
Without your consent.
But your velvet touch engulfed me
with a welcome I didn't expect.
Please. Don't smile too much,
my eyes couldn't bear the beauty.
Just one smile
is enough.
Enough to last an eternity.

Direction Upward Motion

Under ground darkness
Gloomy wet surface

Blindfolded

Naked

Crying all alone
Tears for no one

Terrified

We're all on our own
Merciless
Nothing changes when we're grown
Blocks of ice
Flakes and chunks to the floor
What are you
Reformed
Peculiar looks turning away
Courage is ours to weigh
Procrastinate
Underestimate
Succession will be obtained
Fear will be sustained

Inspire

Rays breaking through
Freedom is sure to ensue

Fallen Leaf

How do we know what we are?
How do we know who we love?
You'll sit alone.
You'll dream, imagine.
If hope is all we have,
we're running out of time.
You think we make choices?
How do we know what to choose?
We accept what is available.
We surrender to life.
We are all broken.
We are all used.
We are fire.
We are water.
Every interaction is a collision.
Pieces of each of us are lost.
We all need glue.
How do we know what pieces to take?
We are forever changing.

Graveyard

wish upon a star
desperate attempt
burned out long ago
night sky holds existence...

desire
her presence magical
fleeting...

passion twinkled
delusions of love
slowly fade
eyes reveal memory.

Imperfect

Open my mind
only to find
an enormous surprise
you didn't see in my eyes.
It's something dark,
an extinguished spark.
Something no longer there
that was once so clear.

An ancient ruin.
An extinct species.
An innocence destroyed.
A rainforest burned.
A cure lost.

Release my hand.
We're running out of sand.
Our love won't last,
I can't turn the hour glass.
I don't want to hold on,
can't you see it's gone.
All that's left is confusion.
What if reality can be my delusion?

A dreamer with no hope.
A holy man with no faith.
A lover with no romance.
An artist with no desire.

Love and the Town of Heartache

I went for a walk the other day.
I happened upon Love.
She saw me,
she smiled.
I asked her where I was.
She told me
I was in the town of
Heartache.
I smiled. She reached out
and grabbed my hand.
She leaned in
towards me.
Her perfume
invaded my senses.
She asked me
if I wanted to grab a cup of
romance.
Her voice
echoed deep within me.
Every syllable weakened my knees.
After the romance,
my body numb,
my mind relaxed,
she thanked me, and
left me
with only her scent.

When I tried to get home
I found all exits closed.
I asked
an old man
if he knew a way out.
He replied,
sorry son,
no way out.
At least you got in.
He smiled
and strolled on.

Weeks later,
while out on a stroll,
I caught a breeze
carrying Love's perfume.
I smiled,
and strolled on.

Our Closest Friend

It's in this familiar setting, everything moving so fast.
So fast.
Everything these eyes see they've seen.
In the window
stares back a transparent face
I
thought I
could know.
He
is the only piece
in this frame
I am unsure of.
He's
just staring at
me.
so sad,
empty.
He must think
the same of me.
The pity on his face,
on mine.

Power of Love

Look inside
my heart. Figure out
the patterns of my kindness.
Scheme
and plan.
Take me
for all I'm worth.
Speak of love
and all it's
wonder.
Mislead
my emotions.
To you
however,
I'm not enough.

Something of a Love

Convincing is the sparkle
in her eye.
It's with her
I want to live
and die. Sweet
is the smell of her hair.
Her skin,
as smooth as cashmere.
Next to me
she'll sleep and
dream,
the companion I've always needed.
The world a brighter place if
every morning
I see her face.
To find such a one,
Where can we look?
To the movies, or a book.
For this feeling,
in reality,
slips away. From each other
lovers fade.
So enjoy
the moments that come along.
It's those memories
you want
to remain strong.

The Music

can you hear the music
as I do?
smile with the melody,
at the harmony?
strangers with smiles
collect around the tables sharing
time. we share this moment
and this life, here sipping,
listening, communicating without words.
slow beat governs the mood
of connection. together in it.
smiling.

Time

the room is empty
as empty as you left it
the windows boarded up
all life dies within
no light shines
cobwebs fill the corners
dust covers the floor

(it is light outside
life moves about)

the room is alone
no way in
no way out

the dust becomes attractive
the webs decorative
the darkness fades
(or all is adapting to it)
it's not so bad in here
no bed no light no life
the door is locked
the best will be made of the gloomy room
for it's all that is known
no more paintings on the wall
no more clothes in the closet
no furniture no color

Time passes unknown

can it be that which saves the room
rotting wood on the windows breaking away
the light has waited long enough
it's taking back what it lost
holes fill with light
the room feels more bright
the wind blows through the rotting wood
the light charges in
taking control of the room
revealing the colors on the wall
the dust is blown from the floors
Life begins to invade
as a bluejay fly's in
she makes the room her home
where she lays her eggs
more animals begin to find shelter
plants grow
the animals know they need each other
the room glows with beauty again

Time passes unknown

What are You Willing to Lose

A treasure: Love.
Now lost.
The masses believe
it can be regained
at the right cost.
Purity, innocence.
Forms these days we lack.
Deceiving eyes,
heart shattering lies.
Always on defense
from those attacks.
Transparent smiles knot our insides.
Dare we open up,
let down our guard,
come out from behind
the mask where our emotions
hide?
Soft embrace of lips
so meaningless.
Taken for granted.
Feelings stolen by greed and
uncertainty.
Moments so
beautiful,
so incredible,
so forgotten.

Lost.

And the hearts
that aren't disguised
pay the cost.

Donor

I'll mend your broken heart.
If pieces are missing
I'll use the broken pieces of my heart.
If you have doubt
I'll fill it with my hope.
If you don't see beauty in the mirror
see it reflecting in my eyes.
Have my eyes,
they only work to see you.
If you're afraid
take my courage.
I'll mend your broken heart...
and lose you forever.

Falling Star

I used to believe that you were a shooting star.
A magnificent vision traveling from the heavens.

How mistaken...

It is I that is the star.
Once glowing with such intensity.
Burned...Unable to withstand...
Falling from hope.
A smear for all to behold.
Granting you substance to wish upon.

Her Cold Front

A bolt of lightning crashes down on my soul,
hail penetrates my skin.
My heart is nothing but charred coal,
blood no longer pumps within.
The storm has taken the best of me,
broken me down to size.
I no longer care for my eyes to see
any more of your lies.
I stand burned, penetrated and exposed.
Always seeing happiness in the distance.
A ballad of pain has been composed
and I no longer want to remain in existence.
Though, perhaps, I'll find another still,
at the end of any hurricane is a brighter world.

In Me

i found my reflection
the puddle of vomit
stare at me
distorted
i saw what was in my heart
gathered crimson
dead calm
exposed
i understand my mind
rorschach painted wall
scattered random
hollow

Love's Consequence

Who are you?
Did I once know?
I never did.
There was always a twist,
it was never solid.
Ignorance was bliss.
We loved.
Did we?
Did you?
I dreamed of love.
How silly I was.
Lost in a movie world,
hoping for that one girl.
Those kisses and smiles,
oh, given to someone else.
I feel like a child.
I still try to believe
in my fantasy, but deep down inside
I know it will never be.
The colors faded.
Why doesn't it hurt?
Am I numb, or worse,
jaded.

Search for Truth

I will find you in the dark
where the world is most harsh.
You will be the only one I see.
I will comfort you, as you comfort me.

The darkness will fade.
The light invade.
Our world will be bright.
Our future right.
Together we shall overcome
the hardships our lives have hung.
Paintings on the wall
remind us of the horrible call
of all our past loves.
Into the light, together we'll fly.
Two doves.
Pure will be our love, and everlasting;
until it ends.

Then light will fade.
Darkness invade.
Separate, alone.
In an empty house
rings our phone.
Never to be answered.
You will need to find someone in the dark
as I found you.
Again you will love, as we once did.

Spring, summer, autumn,
reoccurring like the seasons.
Light to dark,
dark to light.
Comfort lost,
comfort gained.
Everlasting.
Until it ends.

Strangers

These faces walking by,
all unique.
So many stories.
My mind is too weak.
Their eye catches mine,
we share...

Unbelievable.

We share a moment of each others time.
A part of every person that passes,
a shared emotion between all people.
Love, fear, courage, excitement.
We have so much in common
yet we fear conversation.
Diversity is a gift
overlooked.

The Needy

We all want to be something we're not.
Clever, strong, sexy.
We all just wanna be hot!
We want to talk and socialize
but what we really do is hide.
Loneliness feeds off the shy,
so why not just get high?
Marijuana will open you up a bit.
You'll laugh and party the way you wished,
but then you'll wake the next day as you,
the same shy person, what will you do?
You'll look for the new trend
and try to fit yourself in.
You see the girls react to muscles
so you join the gym.
The results you want don't come fast enough,
so once again you turn to drugs.
Now you're big and strong,
respected as a tough guy,
but you're also still, too shy.
Pot no longer gets you where you wanna be
so now you turn to ecstasy.
Since you've gone that far,
try some coke.
Then GHB.

One day the sun will rise.
This is the day you will realize,
doing drugs is a momentary release
and until you're truly happy with yourself
you'll find no peace.

To Fly

There she stands, my salvation.
I'm broken,
lost,
confused,
longing.
And she's there smiling. I forget
what I'm so depressed about.
Everyone,
everything, is so
beautiful.
Flowers in spring, buds bursting
into color
all around. Gigantic
white blotches on a sky-blue canvas.
Warmth.
Birds chirping while newborns
begin to
fly.
There she stands.
Smiling. Tempting.
I step into her direction,
smile,
and begin
to fly.

What's Important

Today I was unhappy.
Lost in fear and doubt.
I need to escape reality,
I need to find an out.
I dream of great achievements,
I awake only to grieve them.
The world turns me off.
A flame to a moth,
how much more do I have to take?
Anger. Hate.
Fear. Fate.
What is real? What is not?
Religion is causing lives to stop.
We need a release and then destroy.
We can't live without our war toys.
More
and more
and more
we consume.
Till there's nothing left to ruin.
Beauty lost, innocence shattered.
A million pieces to the ground scatter.
Bits picked up by onlookers:
LIARS, THIEVES, POLITICIANS, HOOKERS.
All reflections of the world.
Materials.
Materials!

Lose the Madness

I try to think of ways to better life,
a long battle we all have to fight.
I try to figure out all of this madness
and how hate can cause such sadness.

Look around at the world you're in.
The bright green grass,
the blue ocean.
Look up in the sky at the shining sun
and just imagine,
it hits everyone.

We take all of Life's beauty for granted
and when it's gone we're going to miss it.
I too, am guilty of this,
forgetting Life's beautiful gifts.

From now on I'll live a better Life
by not thinking of it as a fight.
I'll lose the madness
and the hate.

Our Journey

Our final moments
This place where peace waits
Dilate
Absorb the light
It will lead you to where most fear
That place where tears are born
Our journey
Inescapable
I will find you there
Walk with you
Soar as one
Live in the dreams that were out of reach
Our brightest hearts illuminate
Battles within will quiet
Victorious in our will
Nothing shall destroy hope

www.ingramcontent.com/pod-product-compliance
Lightning Source LLC
Chambersburg PA
CBHW020338290526
45785CB00005B/2076